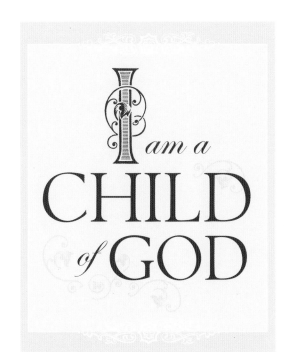

© Greg Olsen. By arrangement with Mill Pond Press, Inc. Venice, FL 34292. For Information on prints by Greg Olsen, please contact Mill Pond Press 1-800-535-0331.

Cover design copyrighted 2001 by Covenant Communications, Inc.

Published by Covenant Communications, Inc.
American Fork, Utah

Printed in China
First Printing: October 2001

08 07 06 05 04 03 02 01   10 9 8 7 6 5 4 3 2

ISBN 1-57734-933-4

Nelsen, Wendy,
    I am child of god/ text by Wendy & Michael Nelsen; artwork by Greg Olsen.
        p. cm.
        Summary: Example of God's love include listening, sharing, and talents.
    ISBN 1-57734-933-4
    Olsen, Greg, ill. III. Title
BX8643.C56 N45 2001
242'.62--dc21   2001042297
                    CIP

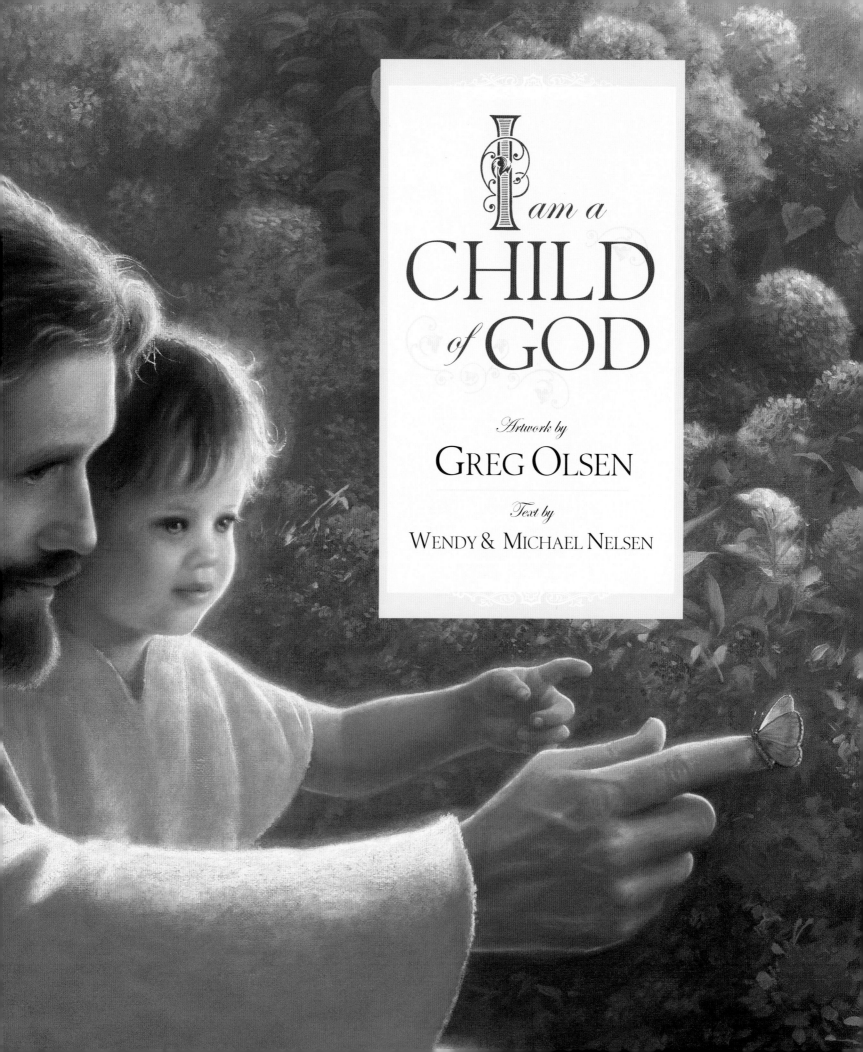

I am a
CHILD
of GOD

Artwork by

GREG OLSEN

Text by

WENDY & MICHAEL NELSEN

I am a

child of God,

so He shares

His love with me.

I am happy

when I share

with others.

know

God listens to me

because

I am His child.

I am a

child of God

and He sees me

as I can

become.

know

I am a child of God

because

He surrounds me

with people who

love me and

keep me safe.

Because I am

a child of God,

I can learn

about His world,

and share

what I learn

with others.

I am a

child of God

and His angels

watch

over me.

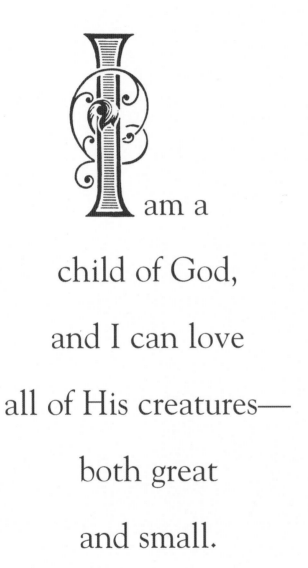 am a

child of God,

and I can love

all of His creatures—

both great

and small.

Because I am God's child, He shows me the way to my dreams.

I am a child of God, and He wants me to choose friends who will help me climb higher.

Because God

loves and cares

for me,

I can learn

to care

for others.

I am God's child, and He has given me a wonderful world to explore.

 am a

child of God,

and He gives me

talents to share

with others

to make His world

more beautiful.

I can be brave

and strong,

for as a child of God,

I am never alone.

I am a

child of God,

and Jesus is

my Brother.

They are my friends.

They know

my name and

They love me.

I am a child of God,
And he has sent me here,
Has given me an earthly home
With parents kind and dear.

I am a child of God,
And so my needs are great;
Help me to understand his words
Before it grows too late.

I am a child of God.
Rich blessings are in store;
If I but learn to do his will,
I'll live with him once more.

I am a child of God.
His promises are sure;
Celestial glory shall be mine
If I can but endure.

Lead me, guide me, walk beside me,
Help me find the way.
Teach me all that I must do
To live with him someday.

In loving tribute to Naomi Randall
Oct. 5, 1908—May 17, 2001

Naomi Randall is known by millions of people for the lyrics of the song, "I Am a Child of God."
The paintings and text in this picture book reflect the beauty and
message of her song, which is loved and sung by children and adults alike worldwide.